THE LIBRARY
SONGS & ARIAS

Handwritten note:

paper due May 17th
(1 pg. double spaced)
-analyze a specific performer
[in Waa-Mu, don't choose a
person playing piano & singing)

posture, breathing, diction, jaw
shape

- through Helais, dynamics, etc

COMPILED BY AMY APPLEBY AND PETER PICKOW

WITH SPECIAL THANKS TO DEBORAH HORNE AND MAURA MAY FOR THEIR INVALUABLE GUIDANCE IN THE PREPARATION OF THIS VOLUME.

THIS TITLE HAS BEEN PREVIOUSLY PUBLISHED AS THE LIBRARY OF VOCAL CLASSICS

ORDER NO. AM 91735
US INTERNATIONAL STANDARD BOOK NUMBER: 0.8256.1389.2
UK INTERNATIONAL STANDARD BOOK NUMBER: 0.7119.3851.2

EXCLUSIVE DISTRIBUTORS:
MUSIC SALES CORPORATION
257 PARK AVENUE SOUTH, NEW YORK, NY 10010 USA
MUSIC SALES LIMITED
8/9 FRITH STREET, LONDON W1V 5TZ ENGLAND
MUSIC SALES PTY. LIMITED
120 ROTHSCHILD STREET, ROSEBERY, SYDNEY, NSW 2018, AUSTRALIA

PRINTED IN THE UNITED STATES OF AMERICA BY
VICKS LITHOGRAPH AND PRINTING CORPORATION

AMSCO PUBLICATIONS
NEW YORK/LONDON/SYDNEY

Contents

Lo so che pria mi moro

I vow my heart so troubled

Pancrazio Aniello
(late 18th Century)

Largo assai

mf

p

poco rit.

a tempo

p

Lo so che pria mi mo - ro che a-
I vow my heart so troub-led Would

poco rall.

ver pa - ce_ e ri - sto - ro al cor_ che lan - gue,
glow with peace re - doub - led, To know for cer - tain:

poco rall.

a tempo

mf.

che do-po mor-to an-co - ra quel ben che l'al-ma a-do - ra sa-
That af - ter life had per - ish'd The Love my spir-it cher-ish'd Would

ră_ per me_ sde-gno - so e nie-ghe-rà_ ri-po - so al cor-po e-san-gue, e
still sur-vive un-al-t'ring, Would still in-crease un-fal - t'ring, Be-hind the cur-tain, Would

nie-ghe-rà ri-po-so al cor-po e-san - gue, al cor-po e-san - gue.
still in-crease un-fal-t'ring, Be - hind the cur-tain, Be - hind the cur - tain!

Under the Greenwood Tree

Text by William Shakespeare

Thomas Arne
(1710–1778)

Un - der the green - wood tree Who loves to lie with me, And

tune his mer - ry note, his mer - ry, mer - ry note Un - to the

Here shall he see_ No en - e - my, But win - ter and rough wea - ther,

Here shall he see_ No en - e - my, But win - ter, but

win - ter and rough wea - ther.

Tempo I

Un - der the green - wood tree Who loves_ to lie with

Mein gläubiges Herze frohlocke

My heart ever faithful

Johann Sebastian Bach
(1685–1750)

Je - sus is here;
Je - sus ist da;

A - way with com - plain - ing, A -
weg Jam - mer, weg Kla - gen, weg

way with com - plain - ing faith ev - er main - tain - ing, My
Jam - mer, weg Kla - gen, ich will euch nur sa - gen, mein

Je - sus is here; My heart ev - er faith-ful Sing prais - es, be joy - ful,
Je - sus ist da; mein gläu - bi - ges Her - ze froh - lo - cke, sing, scher - ze

My heart ev - er faith-ful Sing
mein gläu - bi - ges Her - ze froh-

Die Ehre Gottes aus der Natur
"The Glory of the Lord"

Text by Christian Fürchtegott Gellert

Ludwig van Beethoven
(1770–1827)

Die Himmel rühmen des Ewigen Ehre,
Ihr Schall pflanzt seinen Namen fort.
Ihn rühmt der Erdkreis, ihn preisen die Meere,
Vernimm, o Mensch, ihr göttlich Wort!

The heavens praise the Eternal Lord's glory,
Their sound perpetuates His name.
He is praised by the earth, He is praised by the seas,
Hear, oh man, His godly word!

Him-mel un-zähl-ba-re Ster-ne? Wer führt die

Sonn' aus ih-rem Zelt? Sie kommt und leuch-tet und

cresc.

pp   cresc.   f

lacht uns von fer-ne, und läuft den Weg gleich als ein

sf   p   f   f   f

Held, und läuft den Weg, gleich als ein Held.

ff   sf   sf   sf   ff

Wer trägt der Himmel unzählbare Sterne?
Wer führt die Sonn' aus ihrem Zelt?
Sie kömmt und leuchtet und lacht uns von ferne,
Und läuft den Weg gleich als ein Held.

Who bears the heavens' countless stars?
Who leads the sun from out its tent?
It comes and shines and greets us from afar,
And runs its course, even as a hero.

Vieille Chanson
"In the Woods"

Text by Charles H. Millevoye

Georges Bizet
(1838–1875)

22

The Sleeping Princess

Alexander Borodin
(1833–1887)

Hush! hush! With love - ly eyes Closed in sleep, the

Prin - cess lies, By a fair - y charm en - chant - ed,

Doom'd to dream in for - est haunt-ed: Hush! Hush!

dim.

Più mosso

Sud - den on the

rall. *pp* *cresc.*

mf *dim.*

si - lence break - ing, Laugh - ing, shout - ing, mer - ry - mak - ing,

Thro' the gloom the wood-nymphs sweep, Yet they do not break her sleep.

rall.

f *dim.* *rall.* *p*

Tempo I

Pale and wan, as dead she were, Sleeps the Prin-cess ev - er there.

Hush!   Hush!

Più animato

Some do say that on a day A charm-ing Prince, true-

days go by, a - las! Like a dream they seem to

pass, Yet no Prince has ev - er come To in -

vade the for - est's gloom.

Tempo I

Fast a - sleep the Prin - cess lies, Wrapp'd in mys - ter -

Die Mainacht
May night

Text by Ludwig Hölty

Johannes Brahm
(1833–1897)

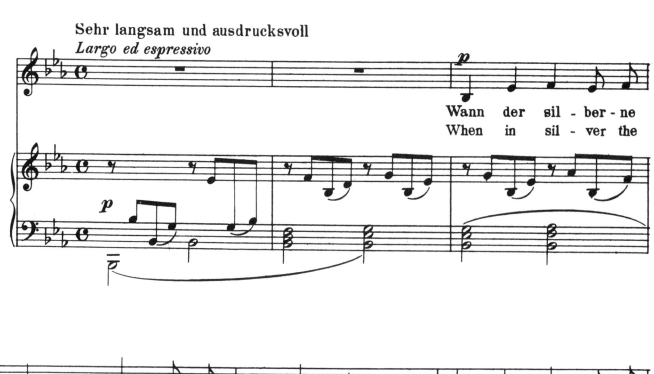

wandl'ich trau - rig von Busch zu Busch.
I go sad - ly from copse to copse.

Ü - ber - hül - let vom Laub gir - ret ein Tau - ben - paar sein Ent - zü - cken mir
Somewhere, hid in the leaves, soft - ly a pair of doves coo their pas - sion to

vor;
me.

a - ber ich wen - de mich,
Yet do I turn a - way,

su - che dunk - le - re Schat - - - ten,
Turn to shades__ that are dark - - - er,

Ständchen

Serenade

Text by Franz Kugler

Johannes Brahms
(1833–1897)

weit _____ und _ breit.
far _____ and _ near.

Ne - ben der Mau - er im Schat - ten da steh'n der Stu - den - ten
Hard _ by the wall in the shad - ow, Three stu - dents have stopp'd and

drei, mit Flöt' __ und Geig' __ und Zi - ther, und
they On lute __ and flute __ and fid - dle Are

sin - gen und spie - len da - bei,_____ sin - gen und
play - ing, and sing as they play,_____ play - - ing, and

cresc.

spie - - len da bei.
sing_____ as they play.

Die
Their

Klän - ge schlei - chen der Schön - sten sacht in den Traum hin - ein,____
mu - sic steals_ to the fair one, And in - to dreams is wrought;____

sie schaut den blon - den Ge -
She sees her gold - en - hair'd

lieb - ten und lis - - pelt: „ver - giss____ nicht
lov - er, And mur - - murs: "For - get____ me_

mein!"
not!"

Meine Lieder

My songs

Text by Adolf Frey

Johannes Brahms
(1833–1897)

Bewegt und leise
Con moto e piano

dolce

Wenn mein Herz be- ginnt zu
When my heart be- gins a-

klin- -gen und den Tö- -nen
rhym- -ing To the mu- - sic

löst die Schwin- gen,
of its chim - ing,

Minnelied
Love song

ext by H. Hölty

Johannes Brahms
(1833–1897)

Bright-er is the bloom-ing Spring, Green-er are its bow-
Rö - ther blü - hen Thal und Au', grü - ner wird der Ra-

-ers, When, with ten - der fin - gers' touch She ____ doth gath - er ____
- sen, wo die Fin - ger mei - ner Frau Mai - en - blu men ____

flow-ers: But for thee all joy were dead, All earth's
la - sen. Oh - ne sie ist al - les todt, welk sind

bright-ness fa - ded. E'en the glow of eve - ning sky Were for
Blüt' und Kräu - ter; und kein Früh - lings-a - bend - roth dünkt mir

La vezzosa pastorella

The lovely shepherd maiden

Domenico Bruni
(late 18th Century)

La_ vez - zo - sa pa - sto - rel - la va co - glien-do in sul_ mat -
In_ the cool and dew-y_ morn-ing Fares the love - ly shep - herd

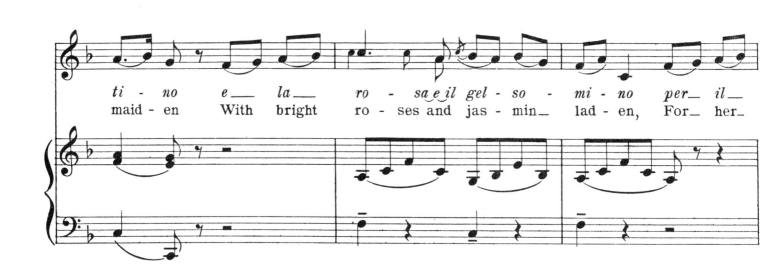

ti - no e_ la_ ro - sa e il gel - so - mi - no per il_
maid - en With bright ro - ses and jas - min_ lad - en, For_ her_

fi - do_ suo pa - stor, va co - glien - do in sul mat -
dear - est_ one de - sign'd; Fares the_ love - ly_ shep - herd

sor, _piú non tro - va il su - o te - sor,_ no, no, non
find! All in vain her love she tried to find. A - las, her

tro - va il su - o te - sor! _La_ _vez - zo - sa pa - sto -_
shep-herd she no-where can find! In_ the_ cool and dew-y_

rel - la va _co - glien - do in sul_ _mat - ti - no e_ _la_
morn - ing Fares the_ love - ly shep - herd maid - en, With bright

ro - sa e il gel - so - mi - no per il _ca - ro_ _suo_ _pa - stor,_ _va co -_
ro - ses and jas - min lad - en, For her dear - est_ one de - sign'd; Fares the

Amarilli, mia bella

Amarilli, my fair one

Giulio Caccini
(c.1550–1618)

Come raggio di sol

As on the swelling wave

Antonio Caldara
(1670–1736)

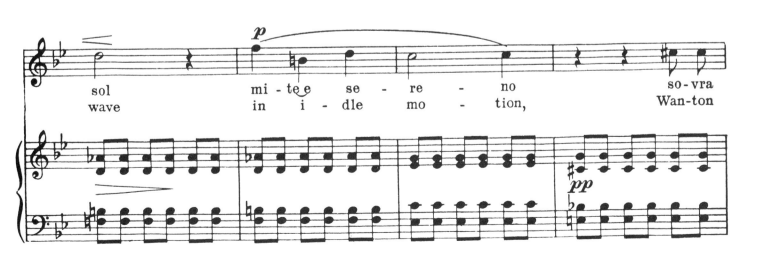

'O sole mio

My sunshine

Text by G. Capurro

Eduardo di Capua
(1864–1917)

Che bel - la co - sa
Oh! what's so fine, dear,

'na iur - na - ta'e so - le,____ n'a - ria se - re - na dop - - po 'na tem -
As a day of sun - shine?____ The sky is clear at last,____ The rain and

pe - - sta!____ Pe' ll'a - ria fre - sca pa - re già 'na fe - sta__
storm are past,____ Thro' air so cool, so bright, Comes the fes - tal sun - light.__

Vittoria, mio core!

Victorious my heart is!

Giacomo Carissimi
(1605–1674)

sciol-ta_ d'A - mo-re_ La_ vil ser - vi-tù, È sciol - - -
love now has bro-ken its_ shack-les in twain, For love_____

- - - - ta d'A - mo-re La ser - vi-tù.
now has bro-ken its shack-les in twain.

meno mosso e dolce assai

Già l'em-pia a' tuoi dan - ni, Fra stuo-lo di sguar-di, Con vez-zi bu -
The false one is van-quish'd, her glanc-es a - muse me, De-cep-tion no

giar - di Di-spo-se_ gl'in-gan - - ni; Le fro-de, gli af - fan-ni Non
long-er with arts can con-fuse_ me! No false-hood or sor-row op -

han - no più lo - - co, Del cru - do suo fo - co È spen - to_ l'ar -
press me with rig - - or, The flame, once so cru - el, has spent all_ its_

Tempo I°

do - - re! Vit - to - ria! Vit - to - ria! Vit - to - ria! Vit - to - ria, mio
vig - - or! Vic - to - rious! Vic - to - rious! Vic - to - rious! Vic - to - rious my

co - - re! Non la - gri - mar più, Non la - gri - mar più, È
heart is! And tears are in vain, And tears are in vain, For

sciol - ta d'A - mo - re La vil ser - vi - tù, È sciol - - - -
love now has bro - ken its shack - les in twain, For love _____

Looking-Glass River

ext by Robert Louis Stevenson

John Alden Carpenter
(1876–1951)

Più animato

Sail-ing blos-soms, sil-ver fish-es, Pa-ven

pools ___ as clear as air ___ How a child

Tempo I°

wish-es To live down there! ___ Smooth it

Les papillons
Butterflies

Text by Théophile Gautier

Ernest Chausson
(1855–1899)

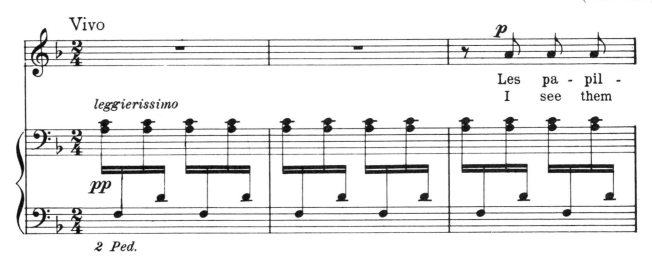

S'ils me vou - laient prê - ter leurs ai - - - -
If they their wings would on - ly lend

les, Di - - - - tes, sa - vez - vous
me, Whith - - - er I would flee,

où j'i - rais? Sans prendre un
dost thou know? With not a

seul bai - ser aux ro - - - ses, A tra - vers val -
kiss to spare the ros - - - es, O - ver vale and

Zwei Leichen

The parted lovers

Text by Bogdan Zaleski

Frédéric Chopin
(1810–1849)

2 There in her own room the faith-ful maid was ly - ing, Far in the
3 High in the church - tower the bells were toll - ing sad - ly, There in the

2 *Drin - nen im Stüb - chen das Mägd - lein lag im Bet - te, doch der Ko -*
3 *Läu - te - ten Glo - cken im Dor - fe von dem Thur - me; heul - ten im*

p legato

for-est wild the Cos - sack youth was dy - ing. Grooped round the maid-en's bed,
for - est the wolves were howl-ing mad - ly; Priests laid the maid-en's form,

sak___ lag an wil - der Wal - des - stät - te. Wein - ten um's Mägd - lein
Wal - de nur Wöl - fe laut im Stur - me. Mägd - lein im Gra - be

poco cresc.

youths and girls la - ment - ed, Fierce o'er the Cos-sack's head ra-vens hung, keen-scent-ed.
in her grave with chaunting While raved the rain and storm, o'er the Cos - sack vaunt-ing.

Mäd - chen wohl und Kna - ben; um den Ko - sa - ken krächz-ten nur die Ra - ben.
deck - te Prie-sters Se - gen; doch den Ko - sa - ken bleich-ten Wind und Re - gen.

dim. *p*

Romance

Text by Paul Bourget

Claude Debussy
(1862–1918)

L'âme é - va - po - rée et souf-
Ev - a - nescent breath of the

fran - te, L'â - me dou - ce, l'âme o - do - ran - te Des lis di - vins__
lil - - y, Ten-der fan - cies, O fra - grant spir - it of heav'nly lays,

__ que j'ai cueil-lis Dans le jar-din de ta pen - sée,
__ Which I in-hal'd 'mid gar-den-ways Of thy dear soul;

Où donc les vents l'ont-ils chas-sée, Cette âme a - do - ra-ble des lis?
Where is it fled on wings of air, Thy soul lil - y-pure, and so fair?

Beau soir
Lovely evening

Text by Paul Bourget

Claude Debussy
(1862–1918)

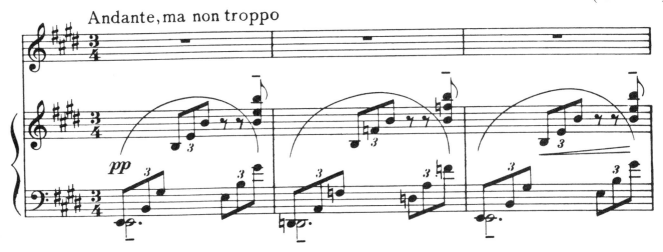

Lorsque au so-leil cou-chant les ri - viè - res sont
When in the set-ting sun ev-'ry streamlet is

ro - - - ses, Et qu'un tiè - de fris - son court sur les champs de
gleam - - - ing, When a trem - u - lous glow spreads o'er the fields of

Les cloches
The bells

Text by Paul Bourget

Claude Debussy
(1862–1918)

Andantino quasi Allegretto

The leaves on the
Les feuil - les s'ou -

green boughs gen-tly are swing-ing, O-p'ning si - lent - ly,
vraient sur le bord des bran - ches, Dé - li - ca - te - ment,

The bells with their mu - sic air - i - ly ring - ing, 'Neath the smil - ing
Les clo - ches tin - taient, lé - gè - res et fran - ches, Dans le ciel clé -

sky.
ment.

Slow - ly breath-ing like an an-them of
Ryth - mique et fer - vent comme une an - ti -

warn - ing, A - far through the air, Bring - ing mem - 'ry
en - ne, Ce loin - tain ap - pel Me re - mé - mo -

sweet of lil - ies a - dorn - ing Ho - ly al - tar
rait la blan - cheur chré - tien - ne Des fleurs de l'au -

fair.
tel.

These bells tell of hap - py years now o'er
Ces clo - ches par - laient d'heu - reu - ses an -

Il pleure dans mon coeur

The tears fall in my soul

Text by Paul Verlaine

Claude Debussy
(1862–1918)

The tears fall in my soul
Il pleu - re dans mon

soul V As the rain on the town.
coeur Comme il pleut sur la vil -

- le, Where - fore creeps this deep
Quelle est cet - te lan -

molto rall.

mad - - - ness,
hai - - - ne,

Still my soul knows such
Mon cœur a tant de

p molto rall.

a tempo

sad - - - ness.
pei - - - ne!

L.H.
R.H.

pp
pp

a tempo
pp

per - den - do - si

pp

e poco rit.

a tempo e morendo
sf > p

pp

L.H.
ppp

pp

Jours passés
Bygone days

Text by Armand Silvestre

Léo Delibes
(1836–1891)

By - gone days! Oh! _____ how soon youth has fad - ed!
Jours pas - sés, O _____ *jeu - nes - se en-vo - lé - e,*

Still I mourn, Sor - row my soul has shad - ed.
Vous lais - sez L'â - me à ja - mais trou - blé - e.

heart hold - eth ev - er Mem - o - ries fond of
front luit en - co - re Ton sou - ve - nir vain-

thee, Ah, mem'ries fond of thee! By - gone days,
queur, ton sou - ve - nir vain - queur! Jours pas - sés.

Molto Lento

Oh! how soon youth has fad - ed, Still I mourn, Sor-
Ó jeu - nes - se en vo - lé - e, Vous lais - sez à

- row has my spir - it o'er - shad - ed, By - gone days, by - gone
- ja - mais mon â - me trou - blé - e, Jours pas - sés jours pas-

Come Again, Sweet Love

John Dowland
(1562–1626)

1. Come a-
2. Come a-

gain,   Sweet love doth now in - vite   Thy
gain,   That I may cease to mourn   Thro'

grac-es that re-frain   To do me due de-light,   To see,—
thy un-kind dis-dain;   For now, left and for-lorn,   I sit,—

Danza, danza, fanciulla gentile

Dance, O dance, maiden gay

Francesco Durant
(1684–1755)

Dan - za,_ dan - za, fan - ciul - la,_ al_ mi - o can - tar; dan - za,_
Dance, O_ dance, maid - en gay, to_ the_ song that I sing; dance, O_

dan - za,_ fan - ciul - la gen - ti - le, al mi - o can - tar.
dance, maid - en_ gay, to_ the_ song, to the song that I sing.

Biblical Song

Antonín Dvořák
(1841–1904)

Sea-Shell

Carl Engel
(1883–1944)

sea - hors - es sta - bled in great green caves. Oh, Sea - shell,

Sea - - shell, Sing of the things you know _____ so

well. _____

Les Rameaux

The Palms

Jean-Baptiste Faure
(1830–1914)

Andante maestoso

Crown ye with palms the Saviour's
Sur nos che-mins les ra-meaux

on - ward way,_____ With branch - es green His ho - ly
et les fleurs_____ Sont ré - pan-dus dans ce grand

path a - dorn, Ho! ev - 'ry one that hath de-sired His day,_____
jour de fê - te, Jé - sus s'avance, il vient sé - cher nos pleurs,_____

Für Musik

For music

Text by Emanuel von Geibel

Robert Franz
(1815–1892)

Now the shad-ows dark-en, Star on stars a-light,
Nun die Schat-ten dun-keln, Stern an Stern er-wacht.

What a breath of long-ing Floods the air at night;
welch ein Hauch der Sehn-sucht flu-tet durch die Nacht.

Through the sea of fan-cy Steer-ing with-out rest,
Durch das Meer der Träu-me steu-ert oh-ne Ruh',

Seeks my soul thy spir - it, Ha-ven, oh,___ how blest.___
steu - ert mei - ne See - le Dei-ner See - le zu.___

Take my heart's de - vo - tion, Thine it is a - lone!___
Die sich dir er - ge - ben, nimm sie ganz da - hin!___

Ah, thou know'st that nev - er I have been my own, have been my own.
Ach, du weisst, dass nim - mer ich mein ei - gen bin, mein ei - gen bin.

Lied
"The Gathered Rose"

Text by Lucien Paté

César Franck
(1822–1890)

Caro mio ben

Thou, all my bliss

Giuseppe Giordani
(1744–1798)

Ca - ro mio ben, cre - di - mi al-men, sen - za di te lan - gui-sce il
Thou, all my bliss, Be - lieve but this: When thou art far My heart is

cor,___ ca - ro mio ben, sen - za di te lan - gui - sce il
lorn.___ Thou, all my bliss, When thou art far_ My_ heart_ is

O del mio dolce ardor

O thou beloved

Christoph Willibald von Gluck
(1714–1787)

L'au - ra che tu re - spi - - ri,
At length the air thou breath - - est

al - fin re - spi - - ro,
my soul in - spir - - eth,

al - fin_____ re - spi - - - -
my soul_____ in - spir - - - -

ro.
eth.
O - vun - - que il guar - - do io
Wher - e'er mine eye_____ may

fp

gi - - ro, Le tue va - ghe sem - bian - ze A -
wan - - der, Still of thee some vague sem - blance Doth

mo - re in me_ di - pin - ge: Il mio pen - sier si fin - ge
Love a - wake with-in_____ me, My ev - 'ry thought doth win_____ me

cresc.

cresc.

Le più lie - - - - te spe -
To yet fond - - - - er re -

cresc.

f

spi - - ri,
breath - - est
al - fin re -
my soul in -

spi - - ro,
spir - - eth,
al -
my

fin,___ al - fin__ re - spi - - - - ro.
soul,___ my soul in - spir - - - - eth.

Ave Maria

Charles Gounod/J.S.Bach
(1818–1893)/(1685–1750)

Ein Schwan

A swan

Text by Henrik Ibsen

Edvard Grieg
(1843–1907)

Andante ben tenuto

My swan, my treas-ure, With
Mein Schwan, mein stil - ler, mit

snow-y-white feath-er, Of his songs sang me nev-er A sin-gle
wei-ssem Ge - fie - der, dei-ne won-ni-gen Lie - der ver-rieth___ kein

meas-ure. Shy-ly fear-ing the
Tril - ler. Ängst-lich sor-gend des

elves in the bush-es. Glid-ed he, list-'ning
El - fen im Grun-de, glittst du hor-chend all-

Ich liebe dich

I love thee

Edvard Grieg
(1843–1907)

Du mein Ge -
Thou art my

dan - ke, du mein Sein und Wer - den! Du mei - nes
thoughts, my pres - ent and my fu - ture, Thou art my

Her - zens er - ste Se - lig - keit!
heart's su - preme, its on - ly joy;

I Know That My Redeemer Liveth

(from *Messiah*)

George Frideric Handel
(1685–1759)

lat - - ter day up-on the earth, _____ up-on the _ earth:

And though worms de-stroy this bod-y,

yet in my flesh shall I see God, yet in my flesh shall I see God.

I know that my Re-deem-er liv-eth,

Love Ye the Lord

George Frideric Handel
(1685–1759)

for He is gra - cious, and will de - liv - er your souls, and give you peace. For __

__ His great mer - cy love __ ye the __ Lord, and He will de - liv - er __ you

from all fear, and give __ you rest to your souls, and give you rest to your

souls.

He Shall Feed His Flock
("Come unto Him")
(from *Messiah*)

George Frideric Handel
(1685–1759)

He_ shall gath - er the lambs with His arm, with_____ His arm,

and car - ry_ them in His bos - om, and

gent - ly lead those_ that are_ with young, and gent - ly_ lead,_ and

gent - ly lead those that are with young. Come_

139

Piercing Eyes

Franz Joseph Haydn
(1732–1809)

Madrigal

Text by Robert de Bonnières

Vincent d'Indy
(1851–1931)

love - li - est eyes?
Dame aux doux yeux!

espress.

a tempo

Where can you find lips ___ more sweet, ev - er smil - ing, Un - to whose
Qui ja - mais eut lè - - vres plus sou - ri - an - tes, Qui sou - ri -

a tempo

p *e molto legato*
(et très-lié)

(a

smil - ing the fond heart re - plies, ___ Or breast more chaste, 'neath
ant ren - dit coeur plus joy - eux, Plus cha - ste sein sous

molto sostenuto
(très-soutenu)

a)

L'Esclave
The captive

Text by Théophile Gautier

Édouard Lalo
(1823–1892)

Che fiero costume

How void of compassion

Giovanni Legrenzi
(1626–1690)

150

Wanderers Nachtlied

Wanderer's night song

Text by Goethe

Franz Liszt
(1811–1886)

The Sea

Text by William Dean Howells

Edward A. MacDowell
(1860–1908)

Élégie

Jules Massenet
(1842–1912)

Ô____ doux prin -
O____ spring of

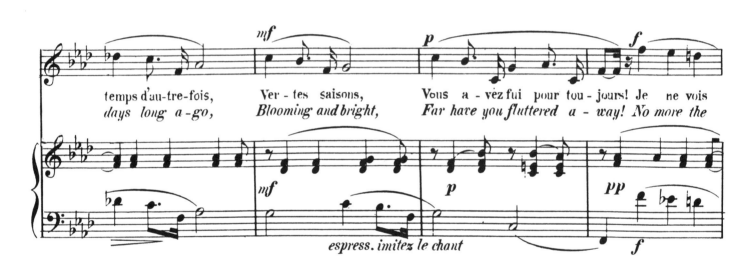

temps d'au-tre-fois,   Ver - tes saisons,   Vous a - vez fui pour tou-jours! Je   ne vois
days long a-go,   Blooming and bright,   Far have you fluttered a - way! No more the

plus le ciel bleu;   Je n'entends plus   les chants joyeux des oi - seaux!   En em-por-
skies' a-zure light,   Car-ol-ing birds   Wa-ken and glis-ten for me!   Bear-ing all

O Rest in the Lord

(from *Elijah*)

Felix Mendelssohn
(1809–1847)

Lasciatemi morire!

No longer let me languish!

Claudio Monteverdi
(1567–1643)

Das Veilchen
The violet

Text by Goethe

Wolfgang Amadeus Mozart
(1756–1791)

Ein Veil - chen auf der Wie - se stand, in sich ge - bückt und
A vio - let on the mead - ow grew, So all a - lone, and

un - be - kannt; es war ein her - zig's Veil - chen! Da kam ein' jun - ge
low - ly too, It was a dar - ling vi - o - let! There came a youth - ful

Schä - fe - rin mit leich - tem Schritt und mun - ter'm Sinn da - her! da und
shep - herd - ess, With step so light, and heart no less, And sang, and

Ave Verum Corpus

Wolfgang Amadeus Mozart
(1756–1791)

It Was a Lover and His Lass

Text by William Shakespeare

Thomas Morley
(1557–1602)

Belle nuit

O lovely night

("Barcarolle" from *Tales of Hoffman*)

Jacques Offenbach
(1819–1880)

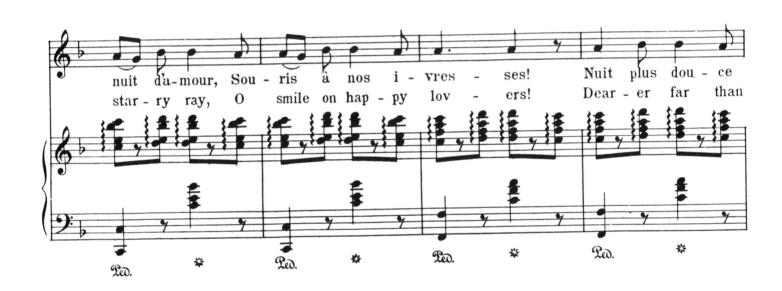

ses, Nuit d'a - mour! ___ ô nuit ___ d'a - mour! ___ Ah!
Love - ly night, ___ O night ___ of love! ___

dim.   pp

ah! ___ ah! ___ ah! ___

ppp

ah! ___ ah! ___ ah! ___ ah! ___

smorzando

ppp

Nel cor più non mi sento

Why feels my heart so dormant

Giovanni Paisiello
(1740–1816)

Nel cor più non mi sen - to   bril - lar la__ gio - ven -
Why feels my heart so dor - mant,   No fire of__ youth di -

tù;   ca - gion   del   mio__   tor - men - to,   a -
vine?   Thou cause of all__ my tor - ment,   O

Se tu m'ami

If thou lovest me

Giovanni Pergolesi
(1710–1736)

m'a - mi,__ se tu so - spi - ri Sol per me, gen - til pa - stor,
lov'st me,__ and sigh - est ev - er But for me, O gen - tle__ swain,

Ho do - lor de' tuoi mar - ti - ri, Ho di - let - to del tuo a - mor, Ma se pen - si
Sweet I find thy lov - ing fa - vor, Pi - ti - ful I feel thy pain. Should'st thou think tho',

178

Passing By

Edward Purcell
(1689–1740)

Andantino moderato

mf espressivo e cantabile   rit.   mp

1. There is a la _ dye
2. Her ges _ tures, mo _ tions

sweet and   kind,   Was ne _ ver   face so   pleas'd my   mind.
and her   smile,   Her wit,____ her voice my   heart_ be _ guile,   Be _

I   did but   see her   pass _ ing   by, And   yet I   love her
guile__ my   heart, I   know not   why, And   yet I   love her

con affetto

Nymphs and Shepherds

Text by Thomas Shadwell

Henry Purcell
(c.1659–1695)

Nymphs and shep - herds, bright and gay, hith - er stray, Hith - er nymphs and
Nymphs and shep - herds, light and free, mer - ry be, Come and join our

shep-herds gay! Come a - way, come, come, come, join our play! To the
jol - li - ty! Laugh and sing, with de - light groves now ring. In sweet

glade, youth and maid, all haste a - way! Sing while we may our roun-de-
bowers, gath - er flowers, all care a - way! Sing while we may our roun-de-

lay! For this is sweet Flo-ra's ho - li - day! This is
lay! For this is sweet Flo-ra's ho - li - day! This is

Flo - ra's ho - li - day! This is Flo-ra's ho - li - day!
Flo - ra's ho - li - day! This is Flo-ra's ho - li - day!

Chanson indoue
Song of India

Nikolai Rimsky-Korsakov
(1844–1908)

Thy hid-den gems are rich be-yond all *mea - sure, Un-num-bered are the pearls thy wa-ters trea-sure, Oh won-drous*

Les di - a - mants chez nous sont in - nom-bra - bles; Les per - les dans nos mers in - cal - cu - la - bles; C'est l'In - de,

Le lever de la lune

Moonrise

Camille Saint-Saëns
(1835–1921)

Ain - si 'qu'u - ne jeu - ne beau - té, Si - len - ci -
As one who is love - ly and young Her lone - ly

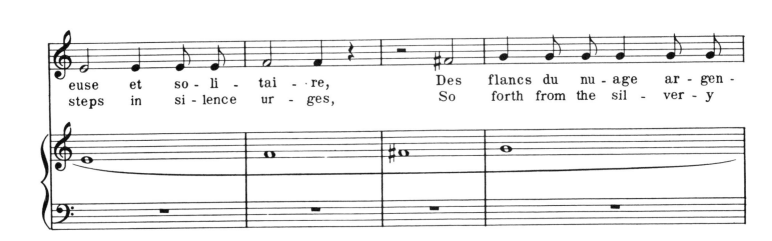

euse et so - li - tai - re, Des flancs du nu - age ar - gen -
steps in si - lence ur - ges, So forth from the sil - ver - y

té La lu - ne sort a - vec mys - tè - re.
clouds The moon in mys - te - ry e - mer - ges.

dolce

Fil - le ai - ma - ble du ciel, à pas lents et sans bruit, Tu
Beau-teous daughter of heav'n, slow thy step, soft and light; Thou

glis - ses dans les airs _____ ou bril - le ta cou - ron - ne;
glid - est thro' thine airs _____ and bright thy crown doth spark - le;

Et ton pas - sa - ge s'en - vi - ron - ne
While round thy state - ly pro - gress cir - cle,

Du cor - tè - ge pom - peux des so - leils de la nuit.
In proces-sion - al train, all the suns of the night.

O cessate di piagarmi

O no longer seek to pain me

Alessandro Scarlatti
(1660–1725)

O ces- sa - te di pia-gar - mi,
O no long - er seek to pain me,

o la-scia - te - mi mo-rir, o la-scia - te - mi mo-rir,
Or give o'er and let me die, Or give o'er and let me die,

Lu- c'in-gra - te, di - spie-ta - te, lu - c'in-gra - te,
Eyes so fate - ful, so un-grate - ful, eyes so fate - ful,

Der Tod und das Mädchen

Death and the maiden

Text by Matthias Claudius

Franz Schubert
(1797–1828)

(♩ = 63)   Tempo I

(DEATH) Give me thy hand, my fair and ten- der
(DER TOD) Gieb dei - ne Hand, du schön und zart Ge -

child, As friend I come, and not to__ chas - ten. Be of good
bild! bin Freund und kom- me nicht zu__ stra - fen. Sei gu - tes

cheer! I bring thee rest; To sleep with - in these fond arms has -
Muths! ich bin nicht wild, sollst sanft in mei - nen Ar - men schla -

ten!
fen!

Morgenständchen

("Hark, Hark! the Lark")

Text by William Shakespeare

Franz Schubert
(1797–1828)

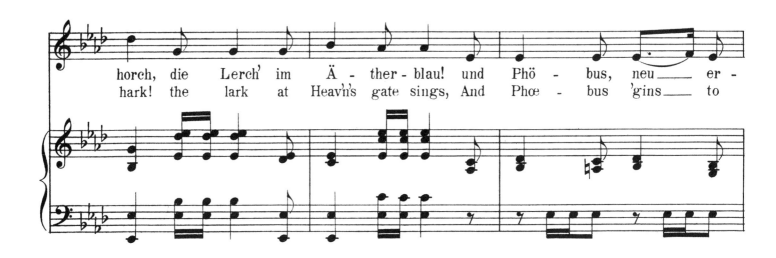

horch, die Lerch' im Ä - ther - blau! und Phö - bus, neu___ er-

hark! the lark at Heav'n's gate sings, And Phœ - bus 'gins___ to

Ständchen
Serenade

xt by Ludwig Rellstab

Franz Schubert
(1797–1828)

Lei - se fle - hen mei - ne Lie - der durch die Nacht zu dir,
Soft - ly goes my song's en - trea - ty Thro' the night to thee,

in - den stil - len Hain her-nie - der,
In - the si - lent woods I wait thee,

Lieb - chen, komm zu mir.
Come, my love,— to me.

Flü-sternd schlan - ke Wip-fel rau - schen in ⏤ des Mon - des Licht,
Tree-tops slen - der sough and whis - per In ⏤ the moon - light here,

pp

in ⏤ des Mon - des Licht, des Ver - rä - thers feind-lich Lau - schen
in ⏤ the moon - light here, No un-friend - ly ear shall lis - ten,

fürch - te, Hol - de, nicht, fürch - te, Hol - de, nicht.
Dar - ling, have no fear, dar - ling, have no fear.

pp

Hörst die Nach - ti - gal - len schla -gen? Ach! sie fle - hen dich,
Hark! the night - in - gales are sing - ing, Ah, they plead with thee!

mit der Tö - ne sü - ssen Kla - gen
With their notes so sweet, so ring - ing,

fle - hen sie für mich.
They would plead for me.

Sie ver-steh'n des Bu-sens Seh - nen, ken-nen Lie - bes-schmerz,
Well they know a lov-er's long - ing, Know the pain of love,

ken - nen Lie - bes-schmerz, rüh-ren mit den Sil-ber-tö - nen
know the pain of love, With their sil - ver-ton-ed voic - es

je - des wei - che Herz, je - des wei - che Herz.
Ten-der hearts they move, ten-der hearts they move.

Lass auch dir die Brust be-we - gen, Lieb - chen, hö - re mich!
Ah, let thine, as well, grow ten - der, Sweet - heart, why so coy?

cresc.

be - bend harr' ich dir ent-ge - gen,
An - xious, fe - ver'd, I a - wait thee,

komm, be - glü - cke mich!   komm, be - glü - cke mich,___
Come and bring me joy,   come and bring me joy,___

be - glü - - cke mich!
and bring me joy!

Ave Maria

Franz Schubert
(1797–1828)

Maid - en hear a maid-en's pray - er, O
ho - ra mor - tis, mor - tis no - strae, in

Moth - er, hear a suppliant child! A - ve Ma-ri -
ho - ra mor-tis no - strae. A - ve Ma-ri -

a!
a!

A - ve Ma - ri - a! Stain - less
A - ve Ma-ri - a! gra - ti-a ple -

styled! Foul de - mons of the earth and
na, Ma - ri - a, gra - ti - a

air _____ From this their wont-ed haunt ex -
ple - na, Ma - ri - a, gra - ti - a__ ple -

iled, Shall flee be - fore Thy pres-ence, Thy
na, A - ve, A - vel Do - mi -

pres - ence fair. We bow un-to ourlot of care__ be -
nus, Do-mi-nus te-cum; Be-ne-di - cta tu in mu-li-e-ri-bus, et

214

Ich grolle nicht
I'll not complain

Text by Heinrich Heine

Robert Schumann
(1810–1856)

I'll not com-plain, tho' break my heart _____ in
Ich grol-le nicht, und wenn das Herz _____ auch

twain.
bricht.

O love for _ ev _ er lost,
E - wig ver - lor - nes Lieb.

O love for _ ev _ er lost! _____ I'll not _____ com -
e - wig ver - lor - nes Lieb, _____ ich grol - - le

Note: The small notes in bars 10, 9 and 8 before the close of the song were not in the original manuscript but were inserted in the engraver's proof by Schumann.

217

Widmung
Dedication

Text by Friedrich Rückert

Robert Schumann
(1810–1856)

heart, Thou both my joy_____ and sad - ness art, Thou art my

Herz, *du mei - ne* *Wonn',_____* *o du mein Schmerz,* *du mei - ne*

heav'n,_____ my match - less lov - er, The world of bliss_____ where - in I

Welt,_____ *in der ich le - be, mein Him - mel du,_____* *da - rein ich*

guid - ing; So has thy love to me ap - peal'd,___ I see my
schie - den: Dass du mich liebst macht mich mir werth,___ dein Blick hat

in - - most self re - veal'd;___ Thou lift - est
mich___ vor mir ver - klärt,___ du hebst mich

a tempo me ___ be - yond my - self; Good gen - ius thou, my bet - ter
lie - bend ü - ber mich, mein gu - ter Geist, mein bess' - res

self. Thou art my life, my soul and heart, Thou both my
Ich! Du mei - ne See - le, du mein Herz, du mei - ne

Separazione
Parting

Giovanni Sgambati
(1841–1914)

Zueignung
Devotion

Text by Hermann von Gilm

Richard Strauss
(1864–1949)

Nur wer die Sehnsucht kennt

None but the lonely heart

Text by Goethe

Peter Ilyich Tchaikovsky
(1840–1893)

From joy and glad - ness.
von al - ler Freu - de!

My sens - es
Es schwin-delt

fail,
mir,

A burn - ing fire de -
es brennt mein Ein - ge -

vours me.
wei de,

None but the lone - ly heart Can
Nur wer die Sehn - sucht kennt, weiss,

know my sad - ness.
was ich lei - de!

Träume
Dreams

Text by Mathilde Wesendonck

Richard Wagner
(1813–1883)

In very moderate time but not dragging
(Sehr mässig bewegt aber nie schleppend)

Sag', welch wun - der - ba - re Träu - - me hal - ten
Tell me what these dreams of won - - der all my

slacken more and more
(immer mehr nachlassend)

wach - sen, dass sie blü - hen, träu - mend spen - den ih - ren Duft,___
flow - ers bloom-ing bright - ly, Soft ex - hale their fra-grant breath.___

p dolce

p

tenderly
(weich)

sanft an dei - ner Brust ver - glü - hen, und dann sin - ken in die Gruft.
On thy bos - om rest - ing light - ly Let them fa - ding. sink to death.

piu p

morendo

pp

piu p

pp

Zur Ruh, zur Ruh!

To rest, to rest!

Text by Justinus Kerner

Hugo Wolf
(1860–1903)

La paloma

The dove

Sebastian Yradier
(1810–1856)

1. The day＿＿＿ that I left Ha - ba - na, (The Lord be praised!)
2. But now＿＿＿ we shall soon be mar-ried, (The Lord be praised!)

1. Cuan - do＿＿＿ sa - li de la Ha-ba-na, ¡Val - ga - me Dios!
2. El dia＿＿＿ que＿ nos ca - se-mos, ¡Val - ga - me Dios!

1-2. If to thy win-dow ev-er shall come a wee dove,
1-2. Si á tu ven-ta-na lle-ga u-na Pa-lo-ma,

Treat it with kind-ness, for thou wilt find 'tis me, love,
Tra-ta-la con ca-ri-ño, que es mi per-so-na,

Tell it thy love, ah! tell it thy love for me, dear!
Cuen-ta-la tus a-mo-res, bien de mi vi-da,

Crown it with flow'rs, be-cause it has come to thee, dear. Do, my dar-ling, I pray!
Co-ro-na-la de flo-res, que es co-sa mi-a. ¡Ay! chi-ni-ta que si,